ASHLIE GILBRET

WEDDING CHECKLIST

The Complete Guide to Planning Your Wedding on a Budget, Discover Effective and Easy Ways to Plan Your Dream Wedding Without Breaking the Bank

Descrierea CIP a Bibliotecii Naţionale a României
ASHLIE GILBRET
WEDDING CHECKLIST. The Complete Guide to Planning Your Wedding on a Budget, Discover Effective and Easy Ways to Plan Your Dream Wedding Without Breaking the Bank / Ashlie Gilbret – Bucharest: Editura My Ebook, 2021
ISBN

ASHLIE GILBRET

WEDDING CHECKLIST

The Complete Guide to Planning Your Wedding on a Budget, Discover Effective and Easy Ways to Plan Your Dream Wedding Without Breaking the Bank

My Ebook Publishing House
Bucharest, 2021

TABLE OF CONTENTS

INTRODUCTION

When it comes to planning your wedding, it's difficult to eliminate some of the features and elements that are most important to you.

With this complete guide to planning the ultimate wedding on a shoestring budget, you won't have to.

In This Ebook You Will Learn:

➢ How To Minimize Costs Without Sacrificing Elements
➢ How to Save Money On All Of Your Wedding Costs
➢ How To Identify Vendors That Are Over Charging
➢ How To Plan Your Wedding From A to Z
➢ Planning The Most Memorable Wedding Day Possible

WEDDING PLANNING ON A BUDGET

Congratulations on your upcoming wedding!

Planning a wedding should be the most memorable experience of your life. After all, you are about to begin a new adventure shared with the one you love.

Unfortunately, when it comes to planning a wedding unless you have an unlimited budget, it can be a frustrating and overwhelming task.

First, you have to determine your budget and then you need to do your best to stay within this amount, which often means cutting corners and eliminating some of the most important elements and features of your day.

Weddings are incredibly expensive if you go the traditional route without knowing how to deal with vendors or negotiate on costs.

With the "Wedding Planning Simplified" guide however, I reveal my personal strategies for saving money on all aspects of your wedding planning as well as how to ensure that your day goes smoothly with little stress involved.

You deserve the ultimate wedding of your dreams, and with my money saving tips and techniques; I truly believe that you will be able to achieve this.

➢ Step One: Determine Your Budget

To begin, you need to sit down with your partner and determine a reasonable budget. Evaluate your finances and how much you are both comfortable with spending on your wedding.

This isn't the time to determine the costs of each element, it's just the taking the first step in your wedding planning and deciding, together, what your wedding fund will be.

The Pre-Planning Phase is a critical step in ensuring that you are organized and on track.

Many couples overlook this very important step, and start planning their wedding without a firm budget in mind. This will make things incredibly difficult when you find yourself out of

10

money and out of time, without the wedding completely planned and ready for your big day.

Sit down together and determine a fair budget. You can always adjust the budget later on down the road if needed, but for now, be open with each other, discuss possible numbers until you come to a reasonable budget without leaving you both struggling to pay off a massive debt once you begin your married life together.

After all, your wedding is a celebration of your love and the last thing you want to do is venture into a marriage where you are tied down to a debt that will take years to pay off. Consider what your objectives are for the first year of your marriage.

Do you want to put a down payment on a house? Upgrade a home? Take an extended vacation? You will need to thoroughly examine what your budget is going to be while allowing you both the ability to save for your future long after the wedding is over.

It's easy to get excited about your wedding planning and take out huge loans or borrow from friends and family without considering how difficult it may be to pay it back over time.

Consider your friends and family who may be interested in helping with certain aspects of your wedding. Perhaps you have a cousin who is a florist or an aunt who would be more than happy to play piano during your ceremony.

You'd be surprised at just how many costly elements you can eliminate by considering friends and family for certain tasks. Best of all, they will be thrilled that you are involving them in your wedding day!

When considering your budget, keep in mind that the majority of a wedding budget is traditionally spent on the reception. The food, drinks, rentals and venue that you choose will take up a large portion of your budget, depending on the type of food served, the number of guests and whether you are footing the entire bill or having friends and family cook, bake and help out.

Your wedding apparel will take up an estimated 15% of your budget as well, and your photographer and videographer another 10-15% by traditional pricing. You could opt to have a friend video tape the wedding for you, as well as a friend or family member that you trust, taking your photographs. This will save a lot of money on your wedding, however be careful in who you choose as you will never be able to capture your wedding again.

If you find that your budget is far too small, start saving every week by deciding to put a specific amount away. You could open a bank account that is used exclusively for your wedding.

> ### ➤ Step Two: Pre-Planning Phase

In order to begin planning your wedding you will both need to discuss what the most important features and aspects of your day will be.

Depending on religion or lifestyles, you both may have specific elements that you feel must be included, and these can affect the budget so it's critical that you write down the "no bargain" aspects of your wedding that you feel you just can't do without.

If you haven't yet set a wedding date, this is the time to do so. Consider what time of year you should have your wedding (considering the guests and their vacation time or ability to attend based on work), as well as whether you are looking to have a wedding locally or away.

The most expensive months in which to get married are spring, summer and early fall, as well as the Christmas and Valentine's Day holidays. If you have a wedding that takes place in late fall or early winter you will be able to dramatically trim down on costs.

Also consider the day of the week as this will also have an impact on your venue costs. Weddings that take place during a weekday are usually far more affordable than a weekend wedding, where venues are in demand and more couples are trying to secure locations.

Often times, vendors will negotiate on costs if you book during an "off day" because they know they are less likely to fill that spot otherwise.

And finally, the time of day also plays a factor in costs. Generally, weddings that take place earlier in the day will cost less than late afternoon, early evening wedding events.

Try to be flexible with the date you choose especially if it will help you stretch the budget even further, enabling you to save money or spend it on other elements of your wedding day that you might otherwise not be able to afford.

Here are a few other questions you will need to discuss before moving past the pre-planning phase:

✓ How many guests would you like to attend?

Write down all of the friends and family members that are most important to you. (Create your "must attend" list first)

✓ What type of venue would you like to be married in? Would you like an indoor lavish reception, and outdoor garden reception, a smaller intimate reception?

✓ What aspect of your wedding day is most important to you both?

✓ How many groomsmen, bridesmaids and other wedding party members are you looking to have?

✓ Will you have a DJ or a band at your reception? DJ's are usually far more affordable than a band.

✓ Should your wedding have a specific theme, and if so, what?

✓ Will you have a buffet style reception or a sit down dinner?

✓ Will you have an open bar, limited or none at all?

✓ Where would you like to go on your honeymoon?

These are just a few of the many questions that you will need to discuss, and while the budget will be affected depending on your choices, you can always trim down as you need to once you begin planning.

Book off a weekend where you and your partner can discuss your wedding, away from noise and distraction. Jot down ideas, notes and suggestions that you both have about your wedding preparations and what you believe are most important elements.

This is very necessary if you want to understand one another and ensure that you include the features and aspects that will make your day extra special.

Remember, these are general questions regarding your wedding planning that will give you a good idea as what you and your partner envision as the „perfect wedding'. Nothing is written in stone and as you begin to plan your wedding day, you are likely going to end up changing certain features, minimizing some of the unnecessary costs and shaping your wedding day so that it encompasses all of the important elements while weeding out the costly features that aren't as important.

I have seen countless couples surprised at just how many ideas their partner has for their wedding day. Ladies, don't discount your partner and it's likely he has ideas on what he would like to see included just as you do.

It's important that you keep an open mind and listen to each other. Does one want a lavish reception while the other prefers a simple buffet style feast?

Do your best to communicate now before you start planning your big day so that there are few surprises or disappointments later on. Work out any disagreements and compromise where needed. After all, this is a very special day for you both and you should both be a big part in the planning.

> ### Step Three: Get Organized

The most affordable weddings are one that are well organized, well planned and well thought out. If you start planning your wedding without writing down everything that you need, you may overlook an important element that you will need to squeeze into your budget later on, so it's important to keep a detailed task list of everything that you need to get organized.

If you have Microsoft Excel, you will find that it is exceptionally easy to create task lists as well as keep accurate records of everything from contacts, vendors to your guest list (including their phone numbers, addresses, who has responded to your invitations, etc). You can also use Excel to keep an up to date list of gifts received at your wedding so that you can send out thank you notes later on.

If you are not computer savvy, you can purchase a wedding planner, which is a simple notepad that contains envelopes and pockets for important notes and memos. You can find these at your local stationary shop, or you can simply create one with a binder, paper, tabs and separators.

Whenever you talk to a vendor that you are interested in working with, ask for a business card so that you can add it to your planner for follow up. Make sure that you have phone numbers, and contact details for everyone involved in the planning of your wedding including florists, reception locations, caterers, DJ's and photographers.

This organizer will also be a great memory book later on, long after your wedding is over! You could also add your wedding CD and photographs to it, creating a scrapbook keepsake.

When I created my wedding planner I added in a "Diary" which allowed me to reflect back later on, and share my thoughts and feelings with my friends and family. Later on when I had my daughter, I intended on handing it over to her so that she could understand how every bride goes through the nerves, the frustration and the secret fears when planning our wedding.

Refer to your planner frequently and stay up to date on the progress you have made. If you are planning your wedding entirely on your own without the help of a wedding planner, you will find your journal and wedding planning notebook an incredible asset in ensuring that you've covered all bases and that you have a handy list of contacts available whenever you need it.

As your wedding day approaches, you will want to create what is referred to as a "timeline of events". This will contain all of the things that you need to have done, in order, prior to your big day.

Make sure to confirm with vendors and hired help the time frame of each element of your wedding (including reception shifting over into a dance if you choose to have one), and go over the service requirements with each vendor so that you both understand what is expected.

Things To Remember:

Discuss with your videographer and photographer what time of day is best for your photos as well as how long your video will be including what elements you want recorded. Be VERY specific in outlining every aspect that you wish to be captured to avoid disappointment or miscommunication later on. Print a copy of your requirements off and hand to each person prior to your wedding day.

Discuss with your DJ or band how long you wish for them to be present, including any specific songs or music you want played and in what order.

Print off a music sheet including all of your requirements and provide to your DJ or band at least two weeks prior to your wedding to ensure that they are able to play this music as well as give them time to ask any questions they may have well before your wedding day.

Talk to your caterer to get an idea of how long cocktail hour will be (if you are including this) as well as what time your reception dinner will begin and come to a close.

Talk to those transporting you to your wedding and reception to ensure that they are aware of when to expect departure and arrival times, as well as if there are multiple wedding parties being transported in the same vehicle at different times.

Make sure you give yourself plenty of time in the event of an unforeseen delay and remember that weddings and receptions often take longer than expected.

When creating your Wedding Timeline always add in extra time just to be careful. There are many things that can happen unexpectedly and by allocating a bit of extra time to each function, you will always be able to maintain your schedule.

Ceremony Location

So, you've determined the month of your wedding and hopefully a handful of potential dates. The next step is in scouting out locations and seeing what is available as well as the costs.

The first step is to decide whether you intend on having the reception and wedding at the same venue, typically if you do, it will cost far less, however depending on the size of your wedding and the available venues, this might not be feasible for you.

If you do not have a particular church or wedding venue in mind, consider renting a hall for both your wedding and reception to save money. Open the phone book and write down the local venues that are available, calling each first to determine availability and cost.

Hosting your wedding and reception at the same venue also saves time and money by being able to eliminate transportation costs.

Many couples also choose to hold their weddings outside in gardens, beaches or local parks. This can cut down costs considerably, however it's very important to contact your local town hall to determine any restrictions that may be in place as well as any associated costs or fees.

Many couples choose to host their weddings at the homes of relatives, in outdoor gazebos, vineyards and even where you first met. As long as your venue is a place that you both feel connected to and is appropriate for you both, as well as your wedding party (size being a factor), go for it! It doesn't matter where you have your wedding as long as you are both happy with your decision and you can ensure that it can accommodate your wedding guests.

If your ceremony location is too small to include your entire guest list, you can also opt for a private wedding with a fewer number of guests present, and open up your reception site to your entire guest list, so that they can celebrate your wedding with you while allowing you and your partner to have your actual wedding at a site that you both are pleased with.

When it comes to your reception keep in mind that certain vendors will charge you for "un used space". This means that if your guest list is 150 and only 100 show up, you still may be required to pay for the remaining 50 seats. Therefore, it's very important to have a closely estimated number of guests and to discuss with your vendor, prior to reserving the reception site, whether you will be charged for anyone not attending your wedding without prior notice.

The location of the wedding is often debated heavily between couples, and sometimes their family. Often, the couple will want to have their wedding in a non-traditional location while the family of one or both insists that they have it in a church.

It's a tough decision.

On one hand, you want to make your parents happy. But on the other hand, it's your wedding. Ultimately it is your decision where to have your wedding. A wedding held on the beach or by a waterfall is no less valid than a wedding held in a church or synagogue.

If you want to have an Elvis-inspired wedding in Las Vegas or a Star Trek themed wedding on a mock Enterprise bridge, that's your choice! And your wedding will still be just as valid as it would have been if it were held right in front of the pearly gates!

There are a couple of main considerations when choosing a wedding location. First, you should choose a location that your friends and family will be able to reach. If you live in Florida, asking your friends and family to all fly to Las Vegas with you may be out of the question. If you are willing to have a smaller wedding with fewer of your loved ones, that's your choice. But it's something to keep in mind.

Next, it should be relatively close to the location of the reception. If you are holding your wedding on the beach, you might want to hold the reception there, as well. You might rent a nice location near the beach, or have the reception at a nearby hotel. But asking guests to drive 10 miles away for the reception isn't going to make anyone very happy.

A wedding is already a long, tiring event. After the wedding, people will probably be tired and hungry. They need to be put into a relaxing, soothing atmosphere quickly and fed! So remember to locate the wedding and the reception close together.

A great idea for many couples is to have the wedding at the home of a friend or relative. This makes for a homier wedding, and the reception can be held right on the premises. This is certainly easier logistically, but it can also be very romantic to have a wedding at the home where the bride grew up, or the home where the groom's grandparents said their vows!

Wherever you choose, just be sure it suits you both. This is a day you will never forget, and it should be held in a place that will make you both happy. Don't worry about what anyone else says. Choose the place that will make YOU happiest.

WEDDING ATTIRE MONEY SAVING TIPS

As a bride, you are likely already dreaming of the perfect wedding gown. Whether you are interested in a traditional, classic or contemporary style, it's always best to begin your search early on, months before your actual wedding day.

To begin, scour the Internet for wholesale discount bridal shops and wedding magazines to determine the style you are interested in and to get an idea for the price range of each style. As you probably know, every website, every magazine and every offline store will have different prices, sometimes for the very same gown, so it's very important to shop around ahead of time, so you aren't rushed into making a purchase, days before your wedding.

Since its likely that your gown may need alterations, it's yet another reason why you should purchase your gown well in advance.

Remember to take into account your body type, size as well as the time of year you are getting married. If your wedding is in the fall or winter, long sleeves makes sense, or if you are having a summer wedding, a short sleeve or sleeveless would be more in fashion.

Once you have determined the style and type of wedding dress that you are interested in, start price shopping. Begin with searching local bridal shops in your area, as well as online. Most online bridal shops offer a money back guarantee so that if you are not happy with the gown once received, you will be able to return it (unaltered) for a quick refund, but be sure to check through the terms of service and return policy prior to ordering.

You will also want to make sure that if you do order a gown online that the distributor provides Fed Ex or overnight delivery, so that you can easily track where your package is as well as confirm receipt.

The last thing you want is your gown to be lost in transit so always request that a tracking number be provided upon purchase.

If purchasing your dress from a local bridal shop, inquire as to the cost of hiring an in-house seamstress, as it's often far more affordable to hire an outside seamstress for your alterations.

If purchasing a gown isn't important to you, you could opt to rent your dress as well as the tuxedo's and bridesmaid dresses for your wedding party. Check your department stores for tuxedo rentals and inquire as to whether there are any special offers, such as the groom receiving his tux rental for free if the groomsmen rent their tuxedo's there. Tux rentals often include cufflinks, vest, tie and sometimes even shoes so be sure to ask.

Otherwise, search through local thrift shops or outlets for second hand tuxedo's or suits that will save you a fortune while ensuringyour groom and his men look fantastic!

Keep budget in mind when selecting dresses for your bridesmaids as well. While a bridesmaid traditionally will purchase her own dress, keep in mind that weddings can be expensive for bridesmaids and try to find inexpensive options for them. Many internet stores sell inexpensive bridesmaid dresses at discounted rates, and these are a good option as long as they have an acceptable return policy.

If you are purchasing your bridesmaid dresses, be sure to choose something that they can use later on, enabling them to get far more use out of it.

➢ **Money Saving Tip:**

If you have your heart set on a designer gown, consider hiring a local seamstress to create it for you. This can be an easy way to have the wedding gown of your dreams without the hefty price tag attached.

Simply bring in a couple of photos of the gown you like, and discuss options with a local (skilled) seamstress.

When it comes to your veil, you can spice up a low priced veil with an affordable jeweled or tulle tiara to give it a special look, all your own without paying top dollar for a long beaded veil.

Wedding Cake At A Discount

The wedding cake is one of the most important aspects of the wedding reception. The cake will adorn the main table, and guests should marvel at its beauty. The cake will feature prominently in photos of the reception, and it will be the main attraction when the bride and groom cut the cake.

The cake should not only be visually stunning, but it should taste great. Many bakeries focus so much on making beautiful wedding cakes that they seem to forget that the cake will be eaten! You should visit a number of different bakeries, not only to get quotes and look at samples, but also to taste some of their wares. Most bakeries will be willing to give you a taste testing if you call in advance.

Be sure to choose a cake that will appeal to both the bride and groom, not only in appearance, but also flavour. The bride and groom should agree on the type of cake they would like to have, but the bride usually has the final say.

In some cases, there is also a groom's cake. If there is to be both a bride's cake and a groom's cake, they can either choose both together, or they can each choose one separately.

Remember, though, the cake that is usually cut together is the bride's cake, and it should be larger and fancier than the groom's cake.

Sometimes you may be able to get a good deal on a cake by allowing the bakery to give you the cake they choose. Many bakers love to get especially creative, and they are sometimes willing to give you a discount if they can create a cake based on their own vision. These types of cakes are fantastic for their portfolio, and it's rare when they are given free rein to create whatever they want.

Often, a cake that is simply decorated will be cheaper than a cake that requires many hours of work. In that same vein, cakes that are iced in butter cream frosting tend to be less expensive than cakes iced with fondant.

Simple cakes with few fillings will be less labor intensive and therefore cheaper than cakes with special flavors and fillings. Call local bakeries in your area and get price estimates for the number of guests you are having.

More couples are deciding to have smaller, simpler cakes these days. Some couples are letting their parents bake simple cakes for the wedding. It certainly saves money, but it can be disastrous if the cakes don't turn out well. If you're going to allow a relative to bake your cake, be certain they know what they are doing!

A wedding cake can cost several hundred dollars, so it's important to try to save money when you can. Just remember that the cake is one part of the wedding that will be preserved on film, and you want it to be something you will be proud of for the rest of your lives.

> **Money Saving Tip:**

Often, grocery store bakeries will also create wedding cakes at a far cheaper price than local bakeries.

RECEPTION CASH SAVING TIPS

Of all the costs associated with your wedding, your reception can be one of the biggest costs of all, especially if you are renting space or using in house caterers. Discuss what your ideal reception venue would be and then research potential spots in your area, by phoning the venues and asking for prices, availability and included items.

When using caterers that are provided by the venue, you can expect to pay 35% more than if you hire an outside caterer, however there are many venues that require you use their in-house vendors so be sure to ask about this when calling each location.

One great way to begin your research is by using the Internet and scouring through different areas in your location. Quite often, reception halls will post details regarding caterers, availability and pricing and in the event this information isn't available, you can choose to contact the management by email prior to calling, to see if it's feasible for your wedding based on your allocated budget.

Create a listing of potential reception spots paying attention to the following:

Schedule And Availability

Are these locations available for your wedding day?

Cost: Determine whether the price is a flat fee or on a per person basis (flat fees are usually cheaper depending on how many guests are included)

Decorations & Inclusions: Determine whether decorations, including centerpieces, table clothes, flowers, candles and other décor are included in the price.

Capacity: Ask how many guests the venue can accommodate, as well as the various seating arrangements that may be available.

Certain venues can hold more guests depending on whether they include longer tables versus round.

Restrictions: Find out whether there are any specific requirements or restrictions in order to reserve and use the hall. For example, certain venues will not allow candles due to fire hazards and insurance costs, while others will not allow certain seating arrangements for the same reasons.

Catering: Determine whether you are able to bring your own catering service to the venue or if you are required to use their on-site staff. If so, determine the overall costs for your reception. If you must use their staff or recommended caterers, request a full list of available caterers and contact each one individually with your questions.

Parking: Make sure that there is sufficient parking based on the number of guests attending your reception as well as ensuring that there is wheelchair access if required.

Time Frame: You will want to determine how long the venue is available for and more importantly, whether there is another wedding taking place on the same day. This can have a huge impact on how well your reception goes, especially if you are under a time crunch or the venue needs to prepare for an additional reception after yours. If another wedding is taking place on the same day, make sure that it ends or begins two hours after yours, to ensure that you, your partner and your guests have plenty of time to enjoy your event.

If possible, try to choose a venue that hosts **only one wedding a day.**

Once you have explored your options and have a list of potential venues, it's time to get in touch with each one directly. You can choose to do this yourself or delegate it to a close friend or family member.

Write down the list of questions that you have and make sure you cover it all before agreeing to book your reception at any venue.

The list should include:

1) How many staff members are allocated to your wedding?

2) Does the venue provide all seating arrangements including tables and chairs or do you need to rent them?

3) Does the venue contain a dance floor, bar and where will the DJ or band be located?

4) Does the venue contain a bridal room or area where you can change from your wedding gown into your reception outfit after dinner?

5) Is there a minimal hour restriction on your reception? Certain venues will require a 4-5 hour minimum where you pay per hour.

Regardless of the type of venue that you choose make sure that you visit it in person before agreeing to book it! A venue can look significantly different in person than in photos and you really need to get a feel for the location, ensuring that it is spacious enough (or intimate enough based on the number of guests), as well as whether it looks clean, is well maintained,

RECEPTION DINNER BUDGET SAVING TIPS

When you must use an in house caterer, there is not much you will be able to do to save money other than choosing less expensive food items. A buffet tends to be cheaper than a sit down dinner, and a soda only reception is cheaper than a reception with a full bar.

Discuss your options with the venue's caterer prior to finalizing your menu details. Many caterers offer a wide variety of services, ranging from hot and cold appetizers, to buffet or served dinners, your choice of bars and some caterers will even include the cake.

The actual food served can save you money as well. Cheaper dishes such as pasta or chicken can be just as lovely, but less expensive than pricey cuts of meat or expensive seafood dishes.

If you want some of the expensive meat or seafood dishes, work with your caterer to see if they can do a seafood appetizer instead of the main course. Your guests will enjoy mini-crab cakes rather than having them as a meal and you will save money.

Being able to hire an outside caterer will give you a lot of room to compare services and prices. Research caterers in your area; the reception venue should be able to recommend caterers that other brides have used, or you can search on the internet or specialized wedding websites.

Word of mouth is also a great resource – talk to people you know who are newly married, or who have attended weddings recently. Make a list of caterers that you are interested in, and ask them the following:

- **Price per Person** – get an idea of their price per head for a buffet dinner, a served dinner, including/excluding appetizers, with/without a full bar, etc. You want to get a price quote for every scenario to really compare prices to other caterers. Many caterers will supply you with a printout listing of their prices.

- **Staff** – find out how many staff will be in attendance on the wedding date. This is usually dependant upon if your dinner is seated or buffet, if you will need a bartender, and how many guests you are having.

- **Cake** – find out if cake is included with the catering services. If cake is not included, find out if your caterer will charge a fee to cut and serve an outside cake.

- **Bar** – find out if the caterer can provide a bar and alcohol (if desired) and if they will be providing their own bartender(s).

- **Linens** – will the caterer provide table linens? Is there an extra cost for linens for a gift table, etc?

- **Centerpieces** – sometimes a caterer will provide their own centerpieces at no extra charge

- **Alternative meals** – instead of a buffet or seated dinner, are they willing to accommodate a cake and champagne brunch, or an appetizer only event?

When researching your catering options, also take into account if you will be serving alcohol.

Once you have narrowed down your choice of caterers, set up a time with each to see them at an event and to taste their food. Bring your fiancé or another person close to you while tasting, and take notes while you are there.

Choose the caterer that best fits your needs and budget.

PLANNING CATERING FOR YOUR WEDDING

Catering is certainly an important part of the wedding reception. You will want to work closely with the caterer to choose a menu that will work well for both the bride and groom.

You will also need to keep in mind the tastes of any potential guests. Traditionally there would be a couple of different main courses to choose from, but these days you must also keep other dietary requirements in mind. Although you can't be expected to provide for every dietary need, you may need to provide vegetarian alternatives if you know there will be vegetarians at the reception.

Ideally you would want to know well in advance if anyone attending has special dietary requirements. If possible, ask guests to alert you to their needs when they RSVP your invitation.

Discuss these needs with the caterer well in advance so they can make arrangements. Sometimes they will need to make special accommodations, so they need to know about this in plenty of time to set everything up properly.

People will special dietary needs are usually used to bringing their own food to events or to going without, so don't panic if a vegetarian shows up unannounced. It's not the end of the world! But it does help to be prepared in case this happens. It's always a good idea to urge your caterer to at least provide one vegan appetizer so any vegetarians can have something to snack on at the very least.

When choosing appetizers, it's best to pick finger foods that aren't very messy. Guests will probably be wearing very expensive clothing, and you don't want them to have any unnecessary cleaning bills! Foods like barbecue and shrimp cocktail are almost certainly off the menu. Cleaner foods like pâté and finger sandwiches are good choices.

The main course can generally be messier, but remember to have at least two courses to choose from. You and your fiancée may enjoy steak, for example, but you should have a chicken or fish dish for those who don't eat red meat.

Weddings should be focused on the bride and groom, but the other guests should be made to feel as happy as possible. The happier the guests are, the more joyous the day will be for everyone. And that will all be preserved on film forever!

SAVING MONEY ON YOUR FLOWERS

Flowers can be a very expensive part of a wedding. Many people spend hundreds, even thousands of dollars on the flowers for their wedding. But there are some tricks you can use to make sure you get beautiful flowers without spending too much money.

First of all, don't choose roses or other expensive flowers unless you are really certain you want them. Many brides choose roses simply because they believe it is traditional or expected. But these days almost any type of flower is acceptable for a wedding. You can always opt to add cheaper flowers such as carnations into a bouquet with a few more expensive types. Or, you may choose one beautiful flower as an alternative to an entire bouquet.

Be careful with color choice. Some colors of flowers are rare than others, and those colors will be more expensive. Discuss with your florist the prices of different colors, and choose one that is affordable, but also one that will make you happy.

You do need to coordinate the flower colors with other colors in your wedding, so that it certainly a consideration. But the flowers don't have to match the color of the bridesmaid dresses or other elements, as long as they don't clash.

You may be able to use fewer flowers than you think. Some brides go all out, and choose flower arrangements for every table at the reception, and they even have a bouquet for every bridesmaid. But this isn't necessary.

You can talk to your fiancé about the flower arrangements, as well as the maid of honor and the florist. Discuss which arrangements are vital, and which might be left out for the sake of economy.

The most important thing to remember is to make sure you get the flowers you really want. Your wedding day is perhaps the most memorable day of your entire life, and hopefully you will only have one. It should be a day you will remember forever, and ultimately you need to be sure you're getting what makes you happiest.

If you are providing your own centerpieces for your tables you have many options. You can create floral centerpieces out of fresh or silk flowers if you are creating the flowers for the rest of your wedding. If you wish not to have flowers, you can float petals in bowls of water or fill glass bowls with colored beads for a pretty look that is easy on the budget.

Candle arrangements also make lovely centerpieces and can be inexpensive if you buy candles in bulk, on clearance, or using coupons.

If you are not using a florist, you can arrange the flowers yourself. It may be easier to use silk flowers in this situation because they can be arranged far in advance, and they may be purchased at discount or using coupons.

If you do choose to work with a florist, discuss with them the best flowers to use for the season of your wedding. Flowers in season will not only be cheaper, but they will hold up better.

➢ Money Saving Tip:

When hiring a florist, never mention the fact the flowers are for your wedding until the price has been negotiated! The word "wedding" often will cause a hijack in price, so keep that in mind when considering the use of professional florists.

Saving Money On Your Invitations

When it comes to preparing and mailing out your invitations, you will want to try to send them out within 6-10 weeks prior to your wedding with an RSVP date of at least 2 weeks prior (preferably 3-4 so that you can prepare).

This allows for your guests to respond and let you know whether they can make it or not, and gives you time to determine just how many guests are likely to attend, in the event you need to follow up with your reception vendor.

Start by creating a "potential" guest list and then if necessary, weed through the list and determine just how many you can afford to invite. If you are having a sit down dinner, you will need to pay for each plate so keep this in mind when creating your guest list.

Don't feel pressured to invite everyone you know. This is your day and you should invite only those who are most important to you, especially when working within a restricted budget.

Once you have your guest list worked out, you will need to purchase invitations as well as stamps and envelope inserts so that those receiving your invitations can respond indicating whether they are able to attend or not.

When it comes to purchasing your invitations, they will range in price from very affordable for basic invitation packages, to incredibly expensive if you are interested in fancy, customized invitations.

If you have a larger guest list, consider choosing a simple yet elegant design that will cost less per package and may include return envelopes as well.

If you really want to save money, you could create your own invitations by using paper stock and your home computer with printer. You can download gorgeous invitation templates from online websites for little or no cost, or if you are the creative type, you could even design your own invitations using scrapbook elements, although this may take some time if your guest list is a lengthy one.

Check with your local stationary store for affordable card stock, and if printing your own invitations at home, use a high quality laser printer for best results.

> **Money Saving Tip:**

Rather than include a return envelope with a stamp, consider including your telephone number or email address to save on postage costs.

Saving Money On Your Wedding Music

Depending on the type of wedding you are having, you may want to have music played during your wedding as well as the reception and dance. Choosing a DJ is always a far more affordable option than hiring a band unless you know someone who is experienced and willing to do this for you.

If you are having your ceremony in a church or temple, check with them to see if music will be provided and what the fee is for the provided music. Some couples choose to have outside music played, for example a soloist or violinist, at their own expense.

Hiring an outside musician to play music for your ceremony may cost quite a lot of money. If you want to have something special played at your ceremony but would like to save money, check in with your friends and family to see if anyone is an experienced musician and would be able to provide their services for you.

If your ceremony is not being held in a church or temple, but at the same location as your reception, you may be able to have a DJ or band play music for both your ceremony and reception.

A DJ will bring his or her own equipment and music, or you can provide music for them to play. A band can vary from a few people to a stage full depending on the type of band.

In general, a DJ is less expensive than a band because you are only paying one person. If you do not have your heart set on live music, a DJ is a great option because they will provide emcee services along with any music you require.

When contacting your musicians, ask them the following:

- Do you charge a flat rate or an hourly rate?
- How early before the ceremony/reception will you arrive to set up your equipment?
- Do I need to provide any music?
- Do you have the ability to play special songs that we wish to have?
- During the reception will you have a set list, or will you take request?
- May we provide you with a list of songs that we do not wish to be played?

When you have selected the DJ or band that you wish to use, keep the contract with all of your wedding paperwork.

PHOTOGRAPHY AND VIDEOGRAPHY
CASH SAVERS

The photographs and video of your wedding day will be keepsakes that you will treasure forever.

The quality of your media, either photographs or video, is dependant upon the person taking the photos or video as well as the quality of their equipment and developing equipment. Photographers and videographers can be very expensive, even for the cheapest packages they offer.

Some photographers will provide video service, but in general if you wish to have both photo and video you will have to hire two different people.

If you want to have professional photographs, perhaps you can have a friend or family member take video of your wedding. Some couples also choose not to have their wedding recorded on video.

Think about your options and what will be best for your wants and budget.

Research photographers carefully as you would everything else in your wedding. Scour the internet and phonebook, and ask your friends and family. Your reception venue and other vendors may also be able to recommend a good photographer.

When you are contacting a photographer, ask what camera they use to take the pictures. Some photographers will only use digital, some will only use film, and then others will use a combination. Also find out if they have an assistant that will be with them.

Photographers often offer package deals. These usually include some combination of printed pictures, digital pictures and CD's (if the photographer is using a digital camera), photo albums, and hours of service.

Contact several photographers and obtain quotes from them, and then meet with a few of them to view their portfolios. Select a photographer who has a style similar to yours. Maybe you would prefer an artistic sort of album or a posed traditional type.

A good way to save money with a professional photographer is to find someone who uses digital and purchase their cheapest package that includes all of the digital photos on a CD.

If you have all of the photographs on CD without a copyright, you will be able to print them at a printer, online, or using your home computer, and only pay for what you need. Also be aware of the number of hours you will need a photographer.

If you want professional photos of getting dressed in your gown, you may have to pay extra for their extra time and travel.

You may save money if you have a friend or family member take photos throughout the day, and use the professional photographer only for the ceremony and reception.

The same advice goes for a videographer – research your choices well, choose someone with a style similar to your own, and pick the least expensive package that will provide you with what you need.

If you are looking to save as much money as possible, you can investigate other sources to find a photographer and/or videographer.

New companies that are start-ups will often photograph or video your wedding at a very cheap price, because they will be able to use your photos/video in a portfolio.

You can also try to locate students at art schools, colleges, and local community colleges that have an interest in photography or videography. They will be willing to work at a cheaper pay because they are looking to gain experience and good references.

YOUR HONEYMOON ADVENTURE

It seems that the only places people think of when you mention "honeymoon" are Niagara Falls and Hawaii! But there are so many beautiful and exotic locations that can be just as romantic. If you're not a fan of Niagara Falls, don't fret!

If the two of you are big fans of the outdoors, why not plan a camping honeymoon? A quiet mountain cabin near a babbling brook, and evenings by a roaring campfire can be just as romantic as any beach! And if the two of you love beaches, remember that Hawaii isn't the only beautiful location for a romantic honeymoon. There are hundreds of gorgeous beaches in the United States alone, and many of them are much quieter and more romantic than Hawaii!

If you love crowds, Hawaii might be a great choice, but many couples prefer a little more privacy and intimacy than a major tourist location. Look for out-of-the-way beaches that offer more privacy if you think the two of you would like more alone time.

Europe is a popular destination for many couples. There are plenty of romantic tours of some of Europe's most romantic cities. You could spend a week seeing the sights of Paris, Rome, Venice, Madrid, and London.

A cruise is another great idea. If the two of you are big fans of the sea, a cruise might be just what you're looking for! And don't expect to spend all of your time on a boat! Many cruises have several landfall destinations where you can go ashore and spend time shopping and sightseeing.

The honeymoon is something the two of you should both enjoy. If you love the beach, but your fiancé can't stand it, a tropical getaway might not be the best choice. You might be disappointed because you didn't get your dream honeymoon in Barbados, but the two of you will have a much more memorable honeymoon if you compromise and choose a mutually enjoyable location together!

CONCLUSION
FINAL THOUGHTS

Your wedding is one of the most special days of your life and both you and your partner should be able to celebrate your love without the stress that comes with excessive debt from taking out loans to pay for your wedding day.

It's important to think beyond the wedding day, and to begin your married life in a way that enables you both to continue celebrating one another, rather than struggle for years to pay off a loan.

Set your budget and use my tips and strategies to ensure that you stay within this price range when planning out your wedding. You can have a beautiful wedding without spending a fortune in the process, if you take your time, stay organized and on track.

To your happily ever after!

Your Name,

www.WeddingPlanningSimplified.com

WEDDING PLANNING CHECKLIST

Wedding planning can be confusing and overwhelming for a first-time bride. It's a tough job. Even if you have a wedding planner to do most of the work for you, you still need to make some decisions on your own.

6-12 Months before the Wedding

✓ Choose a wedding date.

✓ Determine the overall theme, location, time of day, number of guests.

✓ Reserve the site for the ceremony.

✓ Reserve the site for the reception.

- ✓ Book the official for the ceremony. (Priest, Rabbi, Justice of the Peace, etc.)

- ✓ Determine color scheme.

- ✓ Choose and purchase the bridal gown.

- ✓ Obtain a marriage license, and be sure passports and other documents are in order.

6 Months before the Wedding

- ✓ Book a caterer.

- ✓ Book a photographer.

- ✓ Choose and inform the wedding party.

- ✓ Buy attire for the wedding party.

- ✓ Book musicians or DJ.

✓ Book the videographer.

✓ Book a florist.

✓ Sign up for the bridal registry.

4 Months before the Wedding

✓ Reserve rental furniture and items.

✓ Book a decorator.

✓ Finalist the guest list.

✓ Order invitations.

✓ Plan the rehearsal dinner.

✓ Book a honeymoon suite.

✓ Set up accommodations for guests coming from out of town.

✓ Plan the honeymoon.

- ✓ Buy gifts for each other, the wedding party, and both sets of parents.

- ✓ Buy all shoes, lingerie, and accessories.

- ✓ Select wedding bands and purchase.

2 Months before the Wedding

- ✓ Order a wedding cake.

- ✓ Order decorations and party favors.

- ✓ Book the limousine for the wedding day.

- ✓ Address invitations and send them out.

- ✓ Select your ushers, and a guest book attendant.

- ✓ Select a Master of Ceremonies.

- ✓ Mail out invitations to the bridal shower.

6 Weeks before the Wedding

✓ Keep a list of gifts received for thank you letters.

✓ Keep a list of RSVPs.

✓ Purchase a guest book, ring pillow, garter, toasting glasses, cake cutter, and other accessories for the wedding and the reception.

✓ Send invitations for the rehearsal dinner.

✓ Plan a luncheon for the bridesmaids.

✓ Get together the traditional wedding ensemble of something old, something new, something borrowed, and something blue.

2 Weeks before the Wedding

✓ Check with the caterer to make final decisions about the food and drinks.

✓ Make final arrangements with the official, MC, florist, cake decorator, photographer, videographer, decorator, and all others.

✓ Plan the itinerary for the wedding day.

✓ Have the final dress fittings for the bride and bridesmaids.

✓ Contact guests who haven't sent RSVPs to confirm.

✓ Collect wedding rings.

✓ Meet with the musicians or DJ to give them a list of your music choices.

✓ Make a seating chart and print seating cards.

✓ Pick up tickets for the honeymoon.

1 Week before the Wedding

✓ Meet with the caterer for final arrangements, and to present the final guest tally.

✓ Pack for the honeymoon.

✓ Make arrangements for the honeymoon, including having the gas turned off in your home, arranging for mail pickup, arranging a pet sitter or house sitter, etc.

Rehearsal Dinner

✓ Bring all gifts.
✓ Meet with the wedding party and be sure everyone has their itinerary.
✓ Review seating with ushers.

Wedding Day

✓ Make sure the rings are in order.

✓ Double check marriage license and all permits.

✓ Wear your engagement ring on your right hand.

✓ Go through the itinerary one last time.

Printed by Libri Plureos GmbH in Hamburg,
Germany

9 786069 837443